No Biting

Policy and Practice for Toddler Programs

Gretchen Kinnell
for the Child Care Council
of Onondaga County, Inc.

Redleaf Press
St. Paul, Minnesota

Published by Redleaf Press
a division of Resources for Child Caring
10 Yorkton Court
St. Paul, MN 55117
Visit us online at www.redleafpress.org

Redleaf Press books are available at a special discount when purchased in
bulk (1,000 or more copies) for special premiums and sales promotions. For
details, contact the sales manager at 800-423-8309.

Library of Congress Cataloging-in-Publication Data
Kinnell, Gretchen, 1950–
     No biting : policy and practice for toddler programs / Gretchen Kinnell
for the Child Care Council of Onondaga County, Inc.
       p. cm.
       ISBN 1-929610-19-X
       1. Toddlers—Development. 2. Toddlers—Psychology. 3. Children and
violence. 4. Aggressiveness in children. I. Child Care Council of Onondaga
County. II. Title.
HQ774.5 .K56 2002
649'.122—dc21
                                                                    2002017821

Manufactured in the United States of America

Acknowledgements

We would like to thank Mutual of New York (MONY) for its financial support of this project. MONY has funded projects to benefit child care providers in Onondaga County in the past, and we thank them for their continued support.

We would like to thank AIDS Community Resources in Syracuse, New York, for supplying research and information on HIV/AIDS.

We would like to thank Dr. Gary Johnson, Associate Professor of Emergency Medicine at University Hospital in Syracuse, New York, for information on appropriate first aid for biting.

We would like to acknowledge the commitment of the child care centers and especially the directors who sent their teachers and administrators to participate in the task force. Programs also shared some of their forms for us to adapt for this book. We appreciate their support and encouragement.

Finally, we would like to thank the staff of the Child Care Council for their role in producing this book, with a special thanks to Aeron Teratha.

*To the teachers, caregivers, and administrators
who care for and about toddlers every day.*

Contents

Introduction

People who do not work with toddlers in groups might ask, "How can there be enough to say about biting to fill a book?" "Why would anyone need an entire book devoted to biting in toddler programs?" People who *do* work with toddlers in groups, and in all kinds of early childhood programs, however, never ask these questions. They know without a doubt that biting is a serious, complicated issue. They know because they struggle with it on a regular basis.

At the Child Care Council of Onondaga County in Syracuse, New York, we know it too. We know because we have more calls from programs, providers, and parents about biting than any other issue. No other single issue in programs for toddlers inflames parents and frustrates staff the way biting does. Parents do not want their children to be hit, kicked, or injured in any way by another toddler, but parents are usually understanding and supportive of caregivers as they work to resolve those problems. The reaction to biting, however, is different. Seeing flesh torn by teeth seems so primal, so animalistic, and so frightening that it evokes very strong feelings in adults. We have seen adults cry, curse, threaten, and lose their tempers over biting. Even when parents want to be understanding and try to support caregivers' efforts, that understanding and support often gives way to exasperation as biting continues and it seems that nothing will stop it.

The Child Care Council of Onondaga County's Task Force on Biting

For many years the Child Care Council provided technical assistance to programs and advice to parents on an individual basis. We found that many programs approached biting by trying a string of techniques in rapid succession in an attempt to stumble across something that might work. During these times of trial and error, toddler caregivers often confided that they were not at all prepared to deal effectively with biting. They didn't understand why the toddlers were biting, and they couldn't understand why the biting didn't stop even when they tried a variety of punishments. They felt even more unsure of what to do when biting continued and they faced what they referred to as "biting epidemics."

Many programs and providers felt pressured to expel children who were biting. Directors were caught between the parents and the staff and sometimes between the parents of the child who was biting and the parents of the child(ren) being bitten. Parents called us with complaints of incompetent caregivers and unresponsive directors. Other parents called in anguish because their children were being "kicked out of day care" even before they reached the age of two. And, of course, the toddlers themselves were caught in the middle of struggling programs and angry parents.

As we struggled with these biting calls, we wished we knew of materials we could send to parents, programs, and providers. While we could find many articles, they were usually short, general, and limited to one aspect of biting or to a few suggestions. Some of the advice that was available was questionable; some was ineffective; some was downright cruel. What we were looking for was a comprehensive resource for programs that was based on thoughtful and careful consideration of all the issues related to biting in toddler care and that contained appropriate and effective suggestions for caregivers, parents, and administrators. Since we couldn't find one, we decided to convene a group of experienced toddler caregivers and program administrators to do the thinking, consider the issues, and create the resource we had been looking for.

This group became the Task Force on Biting and consisted of seventeen caregivers and administrators from child care centers and Early Head Start in Syracuse, New York, and surrounding Onondaga County. Over the course of several months in 1998 the members of the task force met regularly and created a process to develop the resource. They began by identifying what the Child Care Council wanted the resource to address. The members of the task force thought they could simply gather current information, add some of their own thoughts, and organize it into a set of useful explanations and suggestions. What they found, however, was that their discussions did not focus on simple explanations or solutions. Instead, they found themselves grappling with important issues that are at the heart of the biting dilemma: How do people look at biting? How do programs make decisions about their practices? How do programs deal with problem situations involving children? How do caregivers and programs respond to parent concerns? How do programs respond to pressure from parents?

As the task force members worked through these issues, they realized that the discussions of the problems were as important as the resulting solutions. The Child Care Council decided to incorporate these discussions into the book so that readers would understand the basis for the explanations, suggestions, strategies, and techniques. We also believe that they will be helpful in guiding readers as they grapple with the biting dilemma.

Describing Biting

To begin with, members of the task force found that the words they used to describe the problem of biting among toddlers shaped the way they thought about the issue. They needed to have a common understanding of biting, and common language for the problem of biting, in order to choose responses and develop policies. As a result, the task force struggled with how to describe or label biting. It is certainly a behavior that is a problem, but it's not exactly like other behavior problems because so many toddlers do it, and because many traditional discipline techniques do not work with biting. Since it is often associated with the toddler stage and since so many toddlers bite, task force members considered referring to it as "normal" or "typical." They felt that both of these words implied something that all children would do, something adults should be looking for as an indication that a child's development is proceeding as it should. Logically, then, a child who didn't bite would be seen as a child who was not on target developmentally. Since that obviously isn't true, the task force didn't want to call biting normal or typical. Task force members then tried thinking of biting from their point of view as child care professionals and found that many of them considered it expected behavior.

Using the word "expected," however, didn't seem to be a very good way to talk about biting with parents. Most parents do not expect toddlers to bite, and it seemed unlikely that parents would want their children in a program that expected biting to occur. Calling biting "expected" seemed to portray it as unavoidable and something to be taken lightly. The task force finally settled on describing biting as a toddler behavior that is "unfortunately not unexpected." This conveys the understanding that while biting is not something teachers or administrators want for the children in their programs and not something they look forward to, good programs are not surprised by biting among toddlers and are prepared to address it.

However you refer to biting in your program, this experience teaches that it's necessary to talk about it among the staff members, until you find words that make sense to everyone. In the process, you may uncover differences in your assumptions about biting, which can make it difficult to reach consensus on a plan to address it.

Assumptions about Biting

Most people (and certainly most parents) see biting as a behavior problem that must be punished. If there is no punishment, then the biter has "gotten away with it," which cannot be allowed. Parents are often infuriated when they see their own child bruised with a bite mark and no evidence of anyone serving time for the crime. They may express shock and disbelief when they ask what happened to the child who bit and learn that the child was told, "We don't bite," and then redirected to another area of the room. Parents and teachers alike may want the child who bit to have to "pay the price" for it, because punishment makes them feel that in at least some small way justice has been served. This places tremendous pressure on teachers and programs to punish biting to the satisfaction of the adults. Programs that are good for children, however, do not use techniques to satisfy adults when those techniques are inappropriate or ineffective with children. And punishment is not an effective response to any kind of behavior problem.

While the task force took the position that biting is never the right thing to do, they also recognized that most of the many reasons toddlers bite are not related to behavior problems. The goal of most teachers and parents is to help toddlers stop biting and learn other behavior. Punishing the child who is biting does not reach that goal. It's that simple. What *is* effective at helping toddlers stop biting? To answer that question, it's necessary to understand why toddlers bite, and then find strategies and techniques that match the child's reason(s) for biting. Only then will the biting stop.

Whatever a program ultimately does about biting will come from the way that program looks at biting. Programs that view biting simply as a behavior problem and try to use punishment are not likely to be successful in dealing with it. Programs that want to deny that biting may occur and that try to hush it up when it does are also not likely to be successful. If programs want to be successful in dealing with biting, they must address it in ways that are appropriate for children, families, and staff members. This is most likely to happen when they understand biting as a behavior related to toddler development, when they focus their efforts on helping toddlers who bite learn different ways of behaving, and when they communicate with parents considerately and frankly. This book is based on that perspective, and we recommend it to you as you work to address the biting dilemma in your program.

How to Use This Book

No Biting is organized into three main sections. The first (chapters 1, 2, and 3) addresses the problem itself: why toddlers bite, how to respond when they do, how to help both the child who is biting and the child who is being bitten, and how to develop a plan to deal with repeated biting. This part of the book will help you handle your foremost concern—the children.

Perhaps just as important in controlling biting, however, is how you talk with parents and other caregivers. The second section of *No Biting* (chapters 4 and 5) contains information on how parents see biting, how to talk with them, and how to respond to their suggestions and demands. It also addresses how biting affects adults other than parents—other staff members, and even members of the larger community.

The final section (chapter 6) focuses on creating policies about biting. We know that programs and providers need to have policies in place *before* biting becomes a problem. To do this, policymakers need the information, the experiences, and the suggestions presented in the first two sections of the book to create policies that will work well for their program, the parents, the staff, and the children.

Members of the Task Force on Biting, Child Care Council of Onondaga County

Jennifer Burns	Cazenovia Children's House
Jackie Gower	Cazenovia Children's House
Gretchen Kinnell	Child Care Council of Onondaga County
Sherry Knepp	Kids Unlimited Child Care Center
Linda Leone	Cazenovia Children's House
Lynne Mathews	Childtime Children's Center 0042
Bev Meloon	SonShine Child Care Center
Nancy Meunier	The Growing Place
Pat Nye	Marcellus Presbyterian Child Care Center
Bonnie Phelps	Child Care Council of Onondaga County
Linda Ricks	Early Head Start
Tania Scholder	Salvation Army Clinton St. Day Care
Bethany Scott	SonShine Child Care Center
Carol Taylor	Early Head Start
Alyce Thompson	Salvation Army Day Care Services
Sherry Abdul Wali	Childtime Children's Center 0042
Deb Warren	O'Brien & Gere Child Care Center
Jean Wells	Marcellus Presbyterian Child Care Center

Why Do Toddlers Bite?

Why *do* toddlers bite?

It may be tempting to say, "I don't care *why* they bite, I just want them to stop." This reaction is certainly understandable, but it won't make the biting stop. Understanding why a toddler is biting is the first step to helping her stop. The strategies you choose to help a child stop biting depend on knowing why she is biting in the first place. Toddlers bite for many reasons, which fall into three broad categories:

1. Developmental issues, such as
- Teething pain or discomfort
- Sensory exploration of the surroundings
- Learning about cause and effect
- Learning through imitating others
- Developing autonomy
- Needing more attention
- Learning to hold on and let go
- Developing sensory integration

2. Expression of feelings, which may include
- Frustration
- Anger
- Tension
- Anxiety
- Excitement
- A reaction to abuse or other physical aggression

3. An environment or program that is not working for the child, for example
- An environment that is too stimulating or not stimulating enough
- A space that is too crowded and does not allow children privacy
- Inappropriate expectations (such as expecting toddlers to share toys or equipment)
- A rigid schedule that does not meet toddlers' needs for food and sleep

It takes thoughtful observation to find out why a particular toddler is biting. Any one or a combination of the above reasons may be involved. These reasons are not a checklist that an adult can look over briefly and decide why a child is biting, but rather a guide to many possibilities. It's only possible to know what's going on with a particular child by carefully watching what happens for her over time. Below we take a look at these broad categories to give you an idea of what signs tell you that a given reason might be behind a child's biting.

Developmental Reasons for Biting

Some toddlers bite because of the pain and discomfort of teething. This is especially true of young toddlers, who may not make the distinction between a teething ring that feels good on sore gums and an arm that feels just as good. It is not usually difficult to recognize when a toddler is biting because of teething; she is most likely gnawing on just about everything.

Toddlers may bite because they are exploring. Toddlers learn about objects and people using all their senses. This means they like to discover how things feel and taste in their mouths. It isn't too surprising when the exploration goes from mouthing to tasting to chomping. Observing this progression will help you know when a toddler is using biting as a way of exploring.

Toddlers may bite because they are learning about cause and effect: "What happens when . . . ?" This natural developmental curiosity may become, "What happens when I sink my teeth into Johnny's arm?" Toddlers who bite while they are learning about cause and effect usually do not appear to be upset before they bite. They also may look quite surprised when the child they were exploring reacts loudly to being bitten.

Toddlers may bite because they are imitating others. Toddlers use imitation as a way to learn. They learn many behaviors from other children, and biting can be one of them. Caregivers often report that they have no biting for quite a while. Then one child bites and, the next thing they know, they have an epidemic. When this happens, usually at least one child is biting in imitation of others.

Toddlers may bite because of their developing understanding of autonomy. They are experimenting with asserting themselves as independent beings. They are making choices and trying to control situations and people. Some toddlers bite to demonstrate this control and to have power over others. It is quite easy to recognize when toddlers are trying to sort out autonomy—just listen for lots of cries of "No!" "Mine!" and "Me do it!"

Toddlers may bite because they want and need more attention. Toddlers who need more attention than they are getting may well notice that biting usually results in lots of attention. They would rather get the attention associated with biting—even if it is not pleasant—than get little or no attention.

Sometimes biting is related to maturation of the central nervous system, which allows toddlers to control the muscles that hold on and let go. At first the muscles that hold on are stronger than the muscles that let go. We see this in potty training, as toddlers learn to "hold it" until they get to the potty and then let go of the urine and feces. Toddlers are also working on emotional holding on and letting go. We see evidence of this in *separation anxiety*, when toddlers struggle with letting go of their parents. Biting can be evidence of learning to hold on and let go on another level. Toddlers are sometimes holding onto the skin of someone else that has "somehow" ended up between their teeth.

Toddlers may bite because they have problems with sensory integration. (Sensory integration is the ability to use our senses to take in, sort out, and connect information from the world around us in an organized way.) Toddlers who have problems with sensory integration may find ordinary movements frightening. They may also have difficulties with motor planning and end up biting someone when that was not what they meant to do. Children who need lots of sensory input may even bite themselves.

Biting as a Way of Expressing Feelings

Toddlers may bite because they are frustrated. This frustration is sometimes related to their lack of language skills. Toddlers are working on language development, but when they know exactly what they want and don't yet have the words to make themselves understood, the frustration can mount and result in a chomp. Toddlers may also become frustrated when they cannot get their way. Toddlers are just barely beginning to develop inner control and, when frustration becomes too great, they may bite.

Toddlers may bite to express their anger. When people or objects don't do what toddlers would like, they can easily become angry. Biting in this situation has been called an "oral tantrum." When toddlers bite out of frustration or anger, you can often see their frustration or anger building before the actual bite occurs.

Toddlers may bite to release tension. When people are under pressure, their bodies can become very tense. Toddlers who become tense may bite to relieve the tension in the mouth and jaw.

Toddlers may bite because they are feeling anxious. When toddlers are feeling insecure, scared, or confused about something at home or in the child care program, they may relieve the anxiety by biting. Many adults also use oral solutions to relieve anxiety—for example, smoking, eating chocolate, or drinking.

Toddlers may bite because they are excited. Some toddlers get so excited they can't contain themselves. In the excitement of the moment, they just might joyously sink their teeth into a body part that is close to them. One little boy seemed to be targeting a particular girl for biting. The staff at the center finally asked him, "Why do you bite Mary?" He jumped up and down, clapped his hands, and blurted out, "I just lub her."

Toddlers may bite as a reaction to a physical act that is happening to them. If toddlers are being abused, they may react by being physically aggressive, which could include biting. If a child in group care is bitten many times, he or she may also begin to bite.

Biting as a Reaction to an Inappropriate Program

Toddlers may bite because they are overwhelmed by too much stimulation. There may be too many toys and materials; the environment may be too noisy; lights may be too bright; the schedule may be too rushed; there may not be enough time to relax. Under these circumstances, toddlers become stressed, and stressed toddlers might bite.

Toddlers may also bite if the program is not stimulating enough. They may become bored if they don't have enough toys, materials, or interaction with adults. Boredom is another kind of stress that leads to conflicts.

Toddlers may bite because the space is too crowded and lacks enough private places to retreat to. Toddlers are infamous for finding all kinds of small spaces to crawl into, but sometimes the room is arranged in such a way that all the children end up on top of each other. When children aren't able to find ways to remove themselves from the group, the stress may result in biting.

Toddlers may bite when the program has inappropriate expectations— for example, if they are expected to share toys and there are no duplicates of popular or newly introduced toys. Toddlers have not usually reached a developmental level where they are able to share toys or use them to play with other children.

Toddlers may bite if the program schedule doesn't meet their needs. When toddlers must wait too long, when they are overtired, or when they are hungry, they are likely to bite. Because toddlers, like all people, have varying needs for food and sleep and have different capacities for waiting, a flexible program that allows toddlers to eat and sleep on their own schedule is more likely to meet most of the children's needs most of the time than will one that is rigid.

Preventing Biting

This list makes it clear why, despite their best efforts, teachers cannot guarantee that there won't be any biting in toddler programs. Toddlers bite for so many reasons that it is not possible to predict or prevent every bite. At the same time, no matter what reason is behind a child's biting, children are likely to bite more if they are under stress or if their needs are not being met in the program. For this reason, teachers' expectations of children, their interactions with children, and the way teachers set up the room environment and the daily schedule can affect how likely children are to bite. This is especially true when one or two incidents of biting expand into a biting epidemic. When environments, schedules, expectations, and interactions don't match toddler development, we can expect to struggle with biting. Not only is biting more likely to occur, but it is also more difficult to respond effectively. The rest of this chapter suggests things you can do to help prevent biting and to make it easier to respond to a child who is biting.

Provide a Supportive Environment

- Have duplicates of new toys and popular toys to reduce frustration.
- Keep popular toys available, but avoid overstimulation by making sure all the toys aren't available to the children at once. Rotate toys, storing some away for a while, and then bringing them back out and putting others away.
- Provide small, private spaces where children can go to be alone. You still need to be able to see them, but they need to feel that they are alone. Spaces under lofts or tables or in shelving units are often popular. Toddlers are working on understanding spatial relationships; that's why they like to try fitting themselves into small spaces.
- Provide several soft areas in the room. Use pillows, rugs, and comfortable upholstered furniture to provide coziness.
- Have safe materials visible and available at the children's level so they can use them without an adult having to get them down or get them out.
- Create a variety of activity centers to discourage toddlers from bunching up in one area. Staff will also need to spread themselves throughout the space; children often want to be where the adults are.
- Keep some of the activity areas and materials that the toddlers find most interesting available throughout the day.

Provide a Consistent yet Flexible Schedule

- Keep the daily schedule consistent, so it is predictable for children. Being able to predict what will come next is empowering.
- Simplify the daily routine, so toddlers aren't asked to transition from one activity to the next too often.
- Within a consistent daily schedule, allow for flexibility to meet children's individual needs. Children need to eat when they are hungry and sleep when they are tired, regardless of whether it's snack or naptime.
- Talk about unavoidable changes in the schedule and be understanding of children's reactions to them.
- Have several times each day when children can go outside.
- Keep waiting time to a minimum. Most teachers believe that waiting time in their program is very short and are surprised when they learn how long toddlers are actually waiting between activities. Try asking an objective person to observe your program and keep track of actual waiting time in minutes. To put

waiting time into perspective, take the number of minutes toddlers must wait, put a zero at the end of it, and reflect on how you would react to that waiting time in that situation. For example, if the actual waiting time between an activity and lunch is seven minutes, consider how you would respond to a seventy-minute wait in a similar situation. And remember, you would be expected to be still, be quiet, and be good during those seventy minutes.

● Take the time to go through the daily routine calmly, and don't rush children through activities or routines.

Provide a Variety of Sensory Activities and Materials

● Provide a wide variety of soothing materials and activities. Have scarves and dress-up clothes that are soft and silky and cleaned often. Have sensory activities such as painting and playdough available every day. The sand and water table should be available to toddlers at least several times a week. If your program doesn't have a sand and water table, you can use small, individual basins.

● Provide many cause-and-effect toys that toddlers can act upon to make them "do something." Musical instruments, busy boxes, pounding boards, and jack-in-the-boxes are all examples of cause-and-effect toys.

● Provide opportunities for toddlers to put collections of small, choking-safe objects (for example, clothespins or jar lids, juice can lids, and so forth) in containers, carry them around, and then dump them out. This is a favorite toddler activity and, if indulged, soon progresses to the point where you can begin to teach them about picking up.

● Instead of planning teacher-directed activities, offer interesting materials and experiences. Observe the children's reactions to the materials and then plan how to further their interest. Offer the same thing over and over, so that children have many opportunities to experiment.

● Offer adult-initiated activities that are spontaneous, short, and optional, such as songs, stories, and finger plays.

● Do not expect toddlers to have formal circle time or to sit in whole-group activities.

Interact with Children Gently and Empathetically

● Show children what empathy looks like and sounds like; model it in your interactions with them.

● Respond positively to children.

● Help children identify and name their feelings. Say things such as, "Mark, you look sad to me. Are you feeling sad right now?" or, "Robin, you look frustrated to me. You really wanted to play with that truck, and Sarah has it."

- Show and tell children how to use language to express feelings and state their needs and wants. Say things such as, "Robin, you can tell Sarah, 'My turn next.' That way she knows you're waiting for the truck."
- Encourage children to comfort themselves by using transitional items such as stuffed animals or blankets brought from home or by sucking their thumb or pacifier (if that is what they already do to comfort themselves).
- Comfort children with soothing voice tones and physical actions such as hugs, a thoughtful hand on a child's shoulder, and back rubs.
- Help children fix mistakes. For example, if a child looks genuinely upset that she hurt another, you can say, "Sammy, you look upset that Lonetta is crying. I wonder if she'd like a hug?" Other possible ways to fix a mistake: helping to rebuild a knocked-down tower, kissing a boo-boo, fetching ice for a bite, saying you're sorry (if this is genuine and comes from the child's own feelings, not as an adult-imposed formula).
- Give attention in a generous and genuine manner.

Despite even the best efforts of the best caregivers to prevent it, biting still (unfortunately) does happen. When it does occur, caregivers must be prepared to respond appropriately and effectively. The next chapter will show you how.

What to Do When Toddlers Bite

What most toddler caregivers want to know is, "What do I *do* when a toddler bites?" Unfortunately, there is no simple answer. Because toddlers bite for a variety of reasons and in a variety of circumstances, there is no "one size fits all" response to biting. The response that will help the child stop biting and keep other children safe is different depending on each child's needs, temperament, and reason for biting.

To determine the best response in a given situation, teachers have to observe children closely to find out why they are biting. While gathering this information, pay attention to the environmental factors that might be encouraging the biting, and try to prevent as many further bites as possible. The next chapter will tell you what to do when you have a pattern of continual biting in your program. This chapter focuses on what to do in the moment, when a child has just been bitten. The immediate response is always the same, whether it's the first time the child has ever bitten or the seventh bite that day.

Whenever you're dealing with biting, you need to act quickly and directly. You want your words, attitudes, and actions to convey a strong message:

- Biting is not the right thing to do.
- You will help the child who was bitten feel better.
- You will help the child who bit learn different, more appropriate behavior.

When you are responding to individual biting incidents, you probably won't see the actual bite—only the aftermath. By looking at the two children, however, you can usually get some idea of the circumstances. For example, children who bite because they are exploring, mouthing, or experimenting with cause and effect may look rather surprised at the outraged cries of their victims. When children bite out of frustration or anger, you might see evidence of their feelings in their voices, facial expressions, or body language. If you see one child triumphantly holding a toy while another child with bite marks on her arm is crying and pointing to the toy, you have a pretty good idea of what happened.

At this point, you have to decide where to go and what to say. Sometimes you will want to separate the children; other times you might want the children to be near each other as you deal with the biting. Separate the children when emotions are still high and you worry that more biting will take place if the children are near each other. When deciding whether or not to separate children, pay attention to the feelings of the child who was bitten:

- If he is scared or worried, separate him from the child who bit him. This can be as simple as positioning yourself between the two children.
- If he is furious and ready to retaliate, move the two children to separate areas to prevent escalation.
- If he is indignant, you might bring both children together so the victim can express his outrage directly.

You can also use the reaction of the child who bit to help decide whether to separate the children. If he is calm, curious, or content after biting, it may be a good idea to have him nearby to see the negative effects of his biting.

If you decide to separate the children, either you must have two caregivers who can each attend to one child, or one caregiver must attend to both children, one at a time. If you are attending to both children, you must decide whom to go to first. Unless the child who bit is in danger of hurting someone else, go to the child who was bitten first. Meanwhile, make sure the child who bit sees the aftermath of the biting as you tend to the child who was bitten. Without being punitive, tell the child who bit, "Stay right here for a minute." The more neutral you can be the better—it's important not to be angry or show other emotions. You're not giving him a time-out or punishing him in some way; you just want him to wait until you can finish interacting with him, once you've cared for the child who was bitten.

Helping the Child Who Was Bitten

Check the bite and give the appropriate first aid (see page 11 for first aid information). Comfort the child. Let the child know you regret that he was bitten. This can be a simple statement such as, "I'm sorry you got hurt." You can also tell the child what he could do to respond to the other child. You don't have to insist that he does it, but it helps the child understand that a response is possible and can give him the language and the confidence to respond appropriately. This can be a short statement such as, "You can tell Tommy, 'No, don't bite me.'"

First Aid for Bites

The Task Force on Biting contacted Dr. Gary Johnson, Associate Professor of Emergency Medicine at University Hospital in Syracuse, New York, for information on treating bites in child care settings. He advises that if the skin is not broken, you don't have to worry about infection. The bite may still hurt quite a bit, however, and you may want to offer to put ice on it. Some programs keep ice in small packs or "boo-boo bunnies" (washcloths folded and tied in the shape of a bunny to hold an ice cube) available for such use. Other programs use frozen sponges, wet paper towels in small sealed plastic bags, frozen teething rings, or bags of frozen vegetables such as peas or corn. The frozen vegetables are very popular because they can mold themselves to the shape of various body parts.

If the skin is broken, you need to clean the wound. Plain water is fine; so is soap and water. Antibiotic ointments such as Neosporin are safe but not necessary. Child care program regulations vary from state to state. Check your state's regulations and your program's policies on the use of over-the-counter ointments before using them. After the bite is cleaned, exposure to open air is optimal. If, however, the child is likely to get dirt on the bite wound, you should cover it.

Be especially concerned when bites break the skin on the top of the hand or on the fingers, because bacteria can easily come into contact with tendons. In this case, a child should be seen by medical personnel. This kind of bite, however, is not an emergency that warrants taking the child to the hospital right away. Simply call the child's parents to recommend that the child see a doctor.

Biting among toddlers is serious enough to adults, but some people inflame the issue by claiming that the human mouth is the filthiest of any. While the human mouth may be as bad, it is no worse than the mouths of animals, according to Dr. Johnson, and the human bite is not more dangerous. We may find it more upsetting, however, because we think of biting as an animal behavior, not a human behavior.

Helping the Child Who Bit

Once the child who was bitten is calm, you can turn to the child who bit. A toddler's attention span is usually quite short, so you want to do this within a minute or two. When you respond to the child who bit, be genuine, brief, and serious. You will respond both verbally and with an action, even something as simple as redirecting the child.

Your verbal response must clearly indicate that biting is not the right thing to do. This is not a time to laugh, snicker, or use any kind of humor. You don't want the child to get the impression that biting is cute or funny. It's important to say briefly and clearly what happened and that the biting was not okay. This is especially helpful for toddlers, because it enhances the language skills they are struggling to develop.

Here are some examples of possible things to say to children who have just bitten another child:

- "You bit him with your teeth. He doesn't like it. It's not okay to bite people." (By adding the words "with your teeth," this response clarifies the word "bit" for very young toddlers.)
- "You bit her, and it hurt her. That's why she's crying. I don't want you to bite anyone."
- "You were so mad when the truck wouldn't work! And you bit Trey. Biting hurts people. I'll help you when you're mad, but you may not bite people."
- "Ana had a toy you wanted, and you bit her to take it away. Biting hurts people, and you can't have toys when you bite people to get them."
- "You bit Alex and hurt him. He was trying to get into your cubby with you. You can tell him, 'No, Alex!' But there's no biting."
- "Oh, dear. You were trying to kiss Lee, but you hurt him with your teeth. Please be careful so you don't bite people."

Avoid using verbal responses that are outrageous, untrue, or frightening for toddlers. Telling a toddler that all her teeth will fall out if she bites, for example, is both unfair to the child (because it is untrue) and ineffective in stopping the biting.

The verbal response is almost always followed by an action response. Again, the action you choose to take must fit the circumstances of the incident. If the biting was a matter of mouthing or exploration, caregivers often demonstrate how to touch without hurting. Demonstrate gentle or other appropriate touches on the child who just bit and on the child who was bitten. Telling and showing children what you *do* want them to do is always more effective than telling and showing them what you *don't* want them to do. Don't insist that the child who bit try out the gentle touches on the child who was just bitten. The timing may not be right. Be sure to put lots of language with your demonstrations. Here are some examples:

- "I'm going to use my fingers to touch your arm. Your arm feels smooth and warm. I don't use my teeth on your arm."
- "You can use your hand to touch LaKeisha's cheek if she wants you to."
- "I'll touch your hand like this so you will know how to touch Libby's hand."

Sometimes caregivers have the child who bit help care for the child who was just bitten. This typically involves getting a wet cloth or holding a "boo-boo bunny" (a washcloth folded and tied in the shape of a bunny to hold an ice cube) on the bite for the other child. While this can be very effective for both children, caregivers need to take their cue from the children, particularly the child who was bitten. It should be up to the child who was bitten to accept or refuse the help; this gives the child at least a small measure of control, which is important after not being able to control being bitten. The child who bit may also balk or refuse to help take care of the bite he just inflicted. Insisting that a child in these circumstances must help take care of the other child is not likely to be very effective. In addition, it isn't very reassuring or comforting to the child who was just bitten to find that he is going to be taken care of by someone who is resistant or belligerent.

A child should never profit by biting. If a child bites to get a toy away from another child, he should not be allowed to keep the toy. Even if the other child quickly forgets about the toy, taking the toy away helps send the message that biting is not the right thing to do. This also helps toddlers learn about cause and effect.

While we want to send the message that biting is not the right thing to do, we also need to direct toddlers to what we *do* want them to do. Another good action to take after responding verbally to a child who bit is redirection—directing a toddler's attention to a different toy, activity, person, or area of the room. Redirection is most likely to work well when it is specific. Telling a toddler, "You need to find something else to do," doesn't work nearly as well as, "This doll needs a ride in the buggy," or, "I see Rhonda getting the fingerpaints out." Fortunately, most toddlers are easily redirected.

In some cases, toddlers may insist on doing what you're pretty sure is going to lead to another bite, or they may continue to do what led to the bite in the first place. When you try to redirect them, they may be resistant. You may want to combine several strategies. For example, you can

- **Acknowledge their feelings (and the depth of their feelings).**
  Say something such as, "You really want to hug Jessie, but she doesn't want you to hug her right now," or "You really want to be in that cubby, but Tyrone is in there right now."

- **Redirect them.**
  Say something such as, "I wonder if Sydney would like a hug?" or,

"Tyrone's in the cubby, but I see an empty place under the loft," or, "Carmen has the blue ball, but I see a big red ball on the floor."

- **Give them choices.**

    Say something such as, "You could see if Sydney wants a hug, or give me a big hug," or, "You could go in that empty space under the loft, or try fingerpainting with Rhonda," or, "You could play with the big red ball, or play at the water table with Seth."

Here is an example of how it might work when you put all three redirection strategies together: "You wish you could stay here and get into the cubby with Joey. But only one person can be in the cubby at a time. You can go in a different cubby, or you can play with the trucks."

These responses help children who have just bitten understand that biting is not the right thing to do and that you will help them learn different, more appropriate behavior.

What *Not* to Do

Because biting is such a problem in toddler programs, adults are always looking for ideas and are willing to try almost any suggestion to deal with it. They often try techniques that they have heard about (but not really thought about), only to discover that these techniques are not very effective. This is frustrating for everyone and often leads to claims such as, "We've tried everything, and nothing works!" Here are some of those techniques, along with explanations about why they are ineffective.

Time-out

One technique that is often suggested or tried with young children in programs is the time-out. Not being allowed to participate in an activity may make sense to adults as a punishment, and it might even serve to eliminate an adult's misbehavior. A time-out makes sense to us as adults because we can connect the punishment to the behavior. Toddlers, however, do not experience a time-out in the same way because they don't make that connection. As Piaget reminds us, the way young children think and reason is different from the way older children and adults think and reason.

Trying to put a toddler in a time-out after biting may be as frustrating for the adult as it is for the child. The toddler can't figure out why the adult is so insistent that he or she sit, and the adult can't figure out why the toddler won't stay in time-out. The end result is a battle between the adult and the toddler.

Some adults want to have time-out be an opportunity for children to think about what they did. Can any of us really imagine toddlers who have bitten thinking to themselves, "Oh, dear. I was frustrated because I don't have the language to express my feelings. I took it out on another child by biting. I hurt this other child, and now I feel very sorry for doing it. I should not do this and will never do it again!"

Caregivers may still protest that a toddler "knows what she's doing is wrong because whenever she bites she goes over and sits in the time-out chair." This was observed in one program where a child of twenty months had been biting. The caregivers had been using time-outs with this child and were frustrated because, while time-outs "seemed to be working," the little girl was still biting. During the observation, the little girl was tussling over a toy with another toddler, a boy of about the same age and size. After a brief struggle, the little girl bit the boy, who promptly let go of the toy. The little girl then took herself to the time-out chair, where she sat playing with the very toy she had bitten to get. After a few moments she got up and returned to the group, still playing with the toy. The caregiver was convinced that the girl realized that biting was bad because she went to the time-out chair voluntarily. The caregiver was frustrated because even though the child had "served time" for her crime, she was still biting.

To the outside observer, it was obvious that the girl had learned that biting was followed by a short sit-down period. Putting herself in a time-out had nothing to do with knowing or caring that she had hurt another child. Rather, time-outs had become part of the biting routine. And we know that routines are very important and powerful to toddlers.

Saying, "How would you like it . . . ?"

Sometimes when toddlers bite, adults say to them, "How would you like it if he bit you?" Variations of this technique include, "Would you want someone to bite you?" or, "Do you like it when people bite you?"

If they respond to these questions at all, most toddlers will say, "No." And truly they *wouldn't* like it if anyone bit them; they *wouldn't* want someone to bite them; and they *don't* like it when people bite them.

Having gotten toddlers to agree that they wouldn't want to be bitten, adults then take the next logical step, which is to say, "Well, then, if you would not want to be bitten, probably the child you just bit didn't want to be bitten either." This makes sense to adults because it is the next logical step. And this is exactly why it doesn't work with toddlers. They don't make that logical step because they don't think logically. Logical thinking is one of the characteristics of older children and adults, and again Piaget reminds us that young children do not think and reason in the same way.

So if you get a toddler to agree that he or she would not want to be bitten, you really can't expect them to make the connection to not biting another child. And because they don't make that connection, your saying, "Would you like it if . . ." is not very effective in stopping the biting.

Lecturing, or Going on a Tirade

Sometimes adults respond to biting by telling the child at length what he did wrong and why (a lecture), or by telling him over and over again, with a lot of emotion, not to do something (a tirade). These are both ineffective in stopping biting behavior. Adults may lecture or go off on tirades because it makes them feel as if they are doing something about the biting. It also can release the tension they feel about the biting incident. (Ironically, toddlers also sometimes bite to release tension. A tirade can be thought of as an adult version of biting.)

Lectures are ineffective because they are usually too long and not given in "toddler-friendly" language. Children lose track of what an adult is talking about very quickly, especially in an emotional situation. They need to hear briefly and clearly what happened, what was wrong, and what to do next.

Tirades are ineffective because the adult's voice and body language frighten or surprise children and the message is usually lost. Remember, adding to children's stress increases the chance that they will bite someone. In some tirades, the word "bite" or "biting" is used so often and with such emphasis that it might actually sound like a cheer urging children on to bite. Here's an example:

"You just bit her. There is no biting here. Biting is very bad. Biting hurts other people. We don't bite. Do you want someone to bite you? Don't bite! Don't bite! Don't bite! Do you hear me? Do not bite!"

Delivered in a loud, passionate voice, the intensity of a tirade can be enough to make anyone—especially a toddler—feel like chomping something. Adults need to be aware that just because they feel better after they have delivered a lecture or tirade doesn't mean that they have affected the biting at all.

3

Handling Ongoing Biting

Isolated biting incidents are difficult enough. Many programs and providers feel overwhelmed when the biting becomes repeated, involves more than one child, or seems to go on and on. When you are faced with patterns of repeated biting, you need to develop a plan that involves observation and reflection and that uses specific strategies and techniques identified and chosen because they are a good match for the pattern you are facing. This chapter will help you develop a plan to cope with biting and carry it out step-by-step.

In order to make a plan, you need to gather some information:

1. Observe the children who are biting.

2. Consult with the parents of the children who are biting.

3. Observe and reflect on your program.

These three steps will help you gain insight into the biting. Without taking all of these steps, you will not be able to tailor your responses to the needs of the children who are biting, and that makes your plan less likely to succeed. Once you have gathered thorough information, you will be able to assess the problem and develop a comprehensive plan to address it.

Observe the Child

Remember that long list of reasons why children bite in chapter 1? Observing the child the minute you realize that you have a biting problem in your program is the first step toward understanding why the child is biting. You will need to keep track of the following information over the course of at least a week in order to have enough details about the child to make a good guess about what might be going on. Only by observing over time, without prejudging, can you begin to see if there's a pattern.

Do the bites always happen at the same time of the day? (Maybe the child is hungry or tired then, or maybe it's an especially chaotic time in your schedule.) Do the bites happen at different times of the day, but always during a transition? (Maybe transitions are especially hard for the child.) Do the bites always happen in one part of the room? (Maybe that part of the room is drawing too many children, or there's a bottleneck there that's leading to frustration.) These, and many other possibilities, will be revealed as you keep track of what actually happens when the child bites. If more than one child is biting, you'll need to keep careful observations for each one.

Whenever a bite occurs, you will be filling out an incident report, which contains some of the information listed below (those items followed by an asterisk). Your observation of the child, however, will go beyond the immediate facts of the incident itself. The observation should include the following:

- When the bites have taken place.*
- Where in the environment the bites have taken place.*
- Whom the child has bitten.*
- What was happening just before each bite.*
- The child's reaction after biting.
- The child's social interaction skills.
- The child's verbal skills.
- The child's motor skills.
- The child's general personality characteristics.
- The child's chronological age.

Once you have a week's worth of observations, look at them to see if you can find any patterns. Biting is almost never a random event; a child almost always bites for a reason. You may be able to find several patterns, perhaps one having to do with the time of the bites, another having to do with who is being bitten, or another having to do with where the child is in the room when he bites. Be sure to notice any times or places where the biting never happens, as well. Often, for instance, caregivers discover that the biting does not happen outside, perhaps because children have more space.

Consult with the Parents

While you are gathering information about the child's biting, you will need to talk with the child's parents. From the incident report, the parents will already know that their child has been biting, but you will want to tell them what you have noticed in your program and ask them what (if anything) they have noticed at home. Ask them if they have any insights into the biting. Ask them if they can identify anything that might be upsetting the child. Allow time and opportunity for them to ask you questions too. You can tell them that you are keeping track of the biting to try to understand what the pattern is; you can also tell them that when you have enough information, you will be making a plan to address the biting. They will probably want to know how you handle the child after he bites, and they will probably need to be reassured that their child really is okay, not a monster! See chapter 4 for more information about talking with parents.

Reflect on the Program

Before you make a plan, you also need to observe your program to find out how well it's working for the children, and particularly for the child who's biting. In what ways might your program be contributing to the biting? Examine your environment, materials, activities, schedule, and interactions with children. You can use the preventive measures mentioned in chapter 1 as a checklist to do this observation and reflection. You might also ask your administrator to come in and help observe.

Objective observation can be extremely difficult. In one program, teachers were frustrated when technique after technique failed to make a dent in the biting, which involved several children. Finally an outside observer asked if there was any time at all during the day when there was no biting. At first the staff answered that there wasn't, but as they went through the daily schedule, they realized that the biting did not occur when the children went outside. The teachers changed the schedule temporarily to go outdoors with the children three times during the day instead of just once. It was a big adjustment, but the biting stopped. The teachers then went on to look at the difference between the classroom environment and the outdoor environment. They realized that the classroom was very crowded, and that children were tripping over each other. They tried changing the room arrangement so children had more space to move about without getting in each other's way. With these changes, the biting stopped even when the children were inside.

Objective observation means being brutally honest with yourself, because the program has such a huge impact on the children. A biting problem can almost always be helped by a change in the program. If, for example, you rarely offer sensory activities or materials such as sand and water play or painting because they are too messy, you are probably not providing adequate sensory experiences for children. Sensory play is one of the most effective tools for preventing biting, and providing many opportunities for sensory play can have a huge impact on biting. In order to help the biting stop, you will need every tool you can find. If you don't like to offer sand and water play, find someone who can help increase your comfort level with this activity. As you discover ways to keep the mess minimal, or easy to clean up, you may be less likely to limit the children's experience. And it's much easier to ask children and families to change their behavior when you have shown yourself willing to look at what you can change.

Develop a Plan

From your observations of the child and your conference with the parents, you can determine a possible reason (or reasons) the child may be biting. Your observation and reflection on your program helps you identify specific areas that may be contributing to the biting. Use the information you have gathered in these three steps to develop an action plan. Write down what you are going to do, specifically, to change your program, and what strategies, specifically, you are going to use with the children. For example, "We need more sensory experiences. The water table will be available every day. Janine will supervise it."

Following are strategies and techniques tailored to some of the specific reasons children bite. To address ongoing biting effectively, you will most likely need to implement program changes as well as specific techniques to help the child who is biting.

Strategies and Techniques Related to Development

Teething

- Check with parents to see what they are doing for their child's teething pain. If they are using a treatment to soothe gums, ask them to bring a supply (with instructions) to use at the program as well. Be sure to consult your state's licensing regulations and your program's policy on the use of over-the-counter medications with children.
- Make sure you have a variety of objects that children can chew on to relieve the pain and pressure of teething. These might include teething toys, frozen foods that are chewy and won't cause choking, and clean cloths that have been frozen.
- Actively encourage toddlers who are teething to bite on these items; you are telling children what you *do* want them to bite rather than telling them that you *don't* want them to bite another child after they've already done so.

Sensory Exploration

- Provide many opportunities for sensory play. Offer supervised sand and water play. Have sensory art materials, such as finger-paints and playdough, available for supervised exploration.
- Give children opportunities to explore a variety of textures, spaces, and places. Provide tunnels, small "forts," and different kinds of surfaces for children to crawl on.
- Since toddlers often explore with their mouths, make sure you have a plentiful and varied supply of toys that they *can* put in their mouths. Have a plan for cleaning such toys: One recommendation is to pick up any toy you have seen a child mouth and set it aside to be cleaned; that's why you need so many of them. The toys are then washed with soap and water and sprayed with a bleach-and-water solution (one part bleach to ten parts water) and left to air dry.

Experimenting with Cause and Effect

- Provide toddlers with plenty of cause-and-effect toys. These include toys and activity books in which the child can make something happen by pushing a button, turning a knob, lifting a flap, pulling a tab, and so on.
- Offer art materials, so toddlers can make colors and designs appear by wielding a brush or marker.
- Help toddlers understand "What happens when . . ." and "What happens if . . ." by describing the cause-and-effect relationships you see a child engaging in. Use phrases such as,

  Look at that. When you moved the paintbrush across the paper, you made all that blue.

  Every time you pull the string, that little door opens and you can see the clown.

- When a child bites, use cause-and-effect words to explain the situation. Make sure that the child does not profit from biting. Do not allow the child to keep a toy that was obtained by biting the child who originally had it. "If you bite someone to get a toy, you can't keep the toy." Also use cause-and-effect statements to describe the painful result of the biting such as, "When you bit Maura, it hurt her and she cried."
- Help toddlers recognize the cause and effect of positive behavior. "When you help me put away the blocks, we can find them and play with them again." "When you got more playdough, Maura could use it, too, and she likes that."

Imitating

- When you suspect a toddler might be biting because he or she is imitating another child, provide lots of examples of other, more acceptable behavior for the child to imitate. Model nurturing, sharing, respectful, polite, and empathetic behavior. Show positive ways to handle anger and frustration. When you say, "I was so frustrated when I couldn't get the jar open," or when you respond to a child who is angry with, "You are so angry with Malik because he took the truck you had," you are giving the child a new behavior to imitate.

Emerging Autonomy

- Toddlers need many opportunities to feel powerful and competent while still being safe. You can help foster the child's sense of having power by structuring choices, letting the child make a choice, and then respecting that choice. Toddlers do best with a simple choice between two alternatives, both of which are acceptable. For example, you can offer the toddler the choice between fingerpainting or using the brushes to paint, or a choice between putting the napkin on the table first or the cup on the table first. When the toddler makes the choice, reinforce the power of choosing and support the choice by commenting, "You decided to put the napkin on first." Then make sure you let the child follow through. Try to provide as many opportunities for choosing as possible, because so often you must place limits on toddlers' behavior to keep them safe.

Need for Attention

- If you think a child is biting to get attention, try giving him lots of attention before he resorts to biting. Give attention freely and lavishly; don't make the child wait, ask for, or earn it. Often the children who need positive attention the most are the ones we are least likely to give it to. Make an effort to notice and comment on all the child's acceptable behaviors—being curious, helping, creating, and so forth. Teach the child who had been biting that other, more positive behaviors are even more likely to get your attention.

Holding on and Letting Go

- Give the toddler lots of opportunities to practice physical holding on and letting go. This can be in the form of two favorite toddler activities, "pick up little things and put them into containers" and "pick up, carry around, and dump." Both give the child the opportunity to practice and enjoy holding on and letting go.
- Work on emotional letting go as well. Help toddlers who are having a difficult time with separations by telling them, for example, "You're so sad when your Daddy has to go. It's hard for you when Daddy leaves. He will go to work, and then he will come back after we play outside."
- Children who are having trouble holding on and letting go may not be able to control and "let go" of urine or feces, so hold off on toilet learning.

Strategies and Techniques Related to Expressing Feelings

Frustration and Anger

- Capitalize on toddlers' desire to imitate by expressing your own frustration and anger with words. Teach the child to say an emphatic "No!" or "Stop it!" to another child who is trying to take a toy or book away from him. Encourage children to say, "I don't like it when . . . ," or, "I am so mad when . . . ." Being able to express feelings with heartfelt words may prevent children from expressing those feelings with their teeth.

- Learn to recognize signs of frustration in the child. When you see a child begin to get frustrated, use redirection to help her out of the situation. For example, a six-piece puzzle may be too difficult. Be prepared to redirect her to a puzzle with three pieces so she can experience success instead of frustration.

Tension

- Observe the child so you will recognize signs of mounting tension.
- Help to relieve tension in the mouth and jaw by gently massaging the joint where the jaw meets the skull (just in front of the ear) with circular motions. Don't, however, just swoop down and begin manipulating the face of a child who is already tense. To be more respectful and effective, approach the child from the front and make eye contact. Begin by gently tracing circles on the back of his hand while using a soft, rhythmic voice to say, "I'm making little circles on your hand." Then gradually move up the arm while saying, "I'm making little circles on your arm." Work up to the shoulders, saying, "I'm making little circles on your shoulder." Finally, move your fingers to the spot you want to massage in front of the ear: "I'm making little circles by your ear."

  Massage is so calming that you may want to do it regularly to get the children in your program used to it. Then when you need to use it to relieve tension that may be a factor in biting, the child will be more likely to accept it.
- Step in to redirect when a child is getting into a potentially tense situation. For example, a child may try to get into a private space that another child is already occupying. If you can help him find another space or another way of meeting his need for privacy, he is less likely to bite.
- Provide more gross-motor activities, such as moving arms, legs, and torso to music to relieve tension.
- Try going outside more often to relieve the tension associated with being in more confined spaces.

Anxiety

- Use your own observations and information from the child's parents to understand why the child may be anxious.
- Provide a calm atmosphere by playing soothing music and giving the child one-on-one attention during the day.

- Make sure there is a place for the child to go to get away from the pressures of the group. This might be a quiet corner with soft pillows, or a "house" just big enough for one (perhaps made out of a big cardboard box).
- Help the child calm himself by allowing him to suck a pacifier or his thumb (if he already does this) or by using a lovey or a favorite blanket from home.
- Give the child plenty of time to eat, make transitions, use the toilet, and so forth, to reduce feelings of pressure.
- Soothe the child at naptime with back rubs and songs.

Excitement

- Encourage toddlers to develop a variety of physical (nonbiting) expressions of excitement. For example, have them clap happily, jump up and down, or dance around and yell, "Yeah!" Do this with them when the occasion calls for excitement.
- Be aware that some children have intense reactions to almost everything. This is part of their inborn temperament, and you will notice that these children seem to react more quickly and with more vigor than other children. When they are excited, this inborn tendency to react intensely may result in biting. During moments of great excitement, you may want to position yourself near them to direct their excitement to one of the appropriate actions.

Shadowing: A Last-ditch Technique

When you have exhausted all other possibilities, you may want to try having someone shadow the child who is biting. Shadowing involves having one staff person stay with the child, positioning herself where she can always intercept a bite. Shadowing requires intense vigilance, but it usually works. The staff person shadowing the child is usually able to redirect the child before biting occurs, showing the child different, more acceptable behavior. This means that instead of biting, the child is going through the day *not* biting, and this can become his new behavior.

You should try a complete plan of other strategies for several weeks, adjusting as needed, before resorting to shadowing. Remember that you are looking for improvement, not perfection. If the biting is lessening, stick with your plan. Changes are stressful for children, and giving up on your plan when it is working can bring biting back.

Because shadowing means that one staff person must be devoted to watching and staying with just one child, it is usually difficult for programs to do. If it is tried before other steps in the problem-solving process, its effect is not likely to be permanent. This is because when shadowing stops, problems that may have been contributing to the biting will still exist, and the biting is likely to start again.

A specific version of shadowing can be used when biting involves two children in particular. When a child repeatedly seeks out a particular child to bite, try bringing the two children together for very closely supervised play—perhaps sensory play at a sand or water table. The adult places herself between the children and supervises, interacting with both children and standing ready to make an intervention if the situation warrants it. This gives both children the opportunity to experience bite-free interaction. Further, it allows the child who has been biting to get positive attention for positive interactions

Implement the Plan

Decide on a length of time to try the plan, allowing enough time to implement the changes and follow them consistently. Usually at least a week or two is needed before you can expect to see significant changes in the children. Write down the timeline and who is responsible for each part of the plan. For example, "We need more sensory experiences. The water table will be available every day. Janine will supervise it." Once you have the specifics of the plan written down, share it with the parents of all the children in the room. (See page 27 for more information about how to do this effectively.)

Then begin the trial period. The plan will need to be followed consistently in order to work. If you plan to offer the water table every day, but then you only manage to get it open once or twice during the week, you probably haven't made a big enough change to impact the biting. This doesn't mean that the change didn't work, but that you haven't really made the change yet. Ask your administrator for support and encouragement during this time. And don't forget to keep observing carefully. You may discover new information about the children who are biting, or about the children who are being bit, or about your program. New information can help you revise or fine-tune your plan so that it keeps working.

Finally, evaluate your progress. At the end of the specified trial period, determine whether the biting has decreased. If it has, celebrate your success and keep going. Don't measure your success by whether the biting has stopped completely; that's probably not a realistic goal. If the number of attempted and actual bites has decreased, the plan is working. The biting will continue to decrease over time if you keep observing children and meeting their needs, and eventually will stop completely.

If the biting hasn't decreased at all, you will need to modify your plan or create a new one. To do that, you will have to look back on your observations during the trial period and think about what seemed to work, and why, as well as what didn't work, and why. You will have to think about what parts of the plan you were able to implement, and what you didn't do quite the way you thought you would. Then modify your plan, taking these insights into account. It's a good idea not to change your strategies completely from one week to the next; rather, keep your plan pretty much the same and fine-tune it to make it work better for you and for the children.

Share Your Plan with Parents

Parents need to know what you are doing about ongoing biting. Sharing your plan openly in a letter indicates to parents your willingness to admit a problem exists and shows them that you know what you are going to do about it. This helps restore their confidence in the program.

On page 27 is a sample letter to parents explaining the plan to address ongoing biting. This sample deals with a hypothetical biting situation. It is designed to help you formulate your own letters based on the plans you develop to deal with the ongoing biting that occurs in your program.

Dear Parents,

As you know, we have been struggling with biting in our toddler room. We are all worried about it, and we know you are frustrated with it. When biting becomes an ongoing problem, our policy is to develop a plan to address it based on observation of the children and our program. We have just completed our plan and want to share it with you.

First, we noticed that most of the biting was taking place when children were crowded in the block area. Second, we noticed that the biting usually started when a child bit out of frustration, and other children responded with biting. Third, when we checked our program, we had to admit that we were not providing many sensory activities, which usually serve to calm and soothe children. Fourth, we noticed that there were never any biting incidents when we went outside.

We used these observations to develop the following plan:

1. We have made two block areas in the room so that children will not be bunched up in one block area. These areas are on opposite ends of the room. We're not sure we'll keep it this way, but we want to try it for now.
2. We are stepping up our language development activities with children who are not able to use words to express their frustration.
3. We have set up water play in little basins on the table. We have also added some squares of velour material (thank you, Mrs. Smith, for this donation) to our dress-up area. These are sensory activities and materials that we need.
4. We are going to go outside one more time per day to increase the amount of time when there is no biting.

We'll be trying these strategies for the next two weeks. During that time we'll keep track of the biting to see if it decreases. Please bear with us. We know that positive actions work much better than negative ones, and we're doing our best to provide them.

We know this has not been a pleasant time for you, and we appreciate your support as we work to stop this biting. If you have any questions, please let us know.

Carmen Espinoza, Teacher

Nancy Jones, Teacher

LaTanya Roberts, Director

Help the Child Who Is Being Bitten Repeatedly

With so much attention focused on the child who is biting, it is easy to forget that the child who is being bitten may also need help. Any time a child is bitten we need to provide first aid, comfort, and reassurance. But when we notice a particular child is being bitten again and again, that child may need more help from us. We don't want children to feel helpless, and we don't want children to become comfortable in the role of the victim. Learning to stand up for oneself is an important social and emotional goal for young children. We also want to help the child who is being bitten repeatedly because that child may respond by biting in return.

First, let the child who is being bitten repeatedly know that it is all right to be mad (or frightened or worried) when someone bites him. You may actually have to tell him, "You don't like it when Mary bites you. She hurt you."

Second, help children learn the language to say "No" when another child is hurting them. This language may range from a simple, emphatic "No!" or "Stop!" to longer phrases, such as, "Don't bite me." Model the words and tone for children to use. It will be much easier for them to learn to stand up for themselves if they can start by imitating your words and tone instead of trying to come up with their own. This also gives you another possibility for preventing a bite: when you hear children using their new words to react to a bite, respond quickly and you may be able to help the children solve a problem before one of them gets bitten.

As with any technique or strategy, you need to base your actions on observations. If you are observing a child who is being bitten a great deal, you may discover that something the child is doing is resulting in her being bitten. An example might be a little girl grabbing a toy right out of the hands of a little boy who then bites her. You don't want the little boy to bite, and you don't want the little girl to be bitten. At the same time, you don't want the girl to take the toy away from the boy. In this case, you need to redirect the girl toward a different toy and help her begin to understand that she may not grab a toy away from someone else. Both children need to learn different behavior.

Working with Parents and Other Community Members

Biting in child care programs can strain even the best relationships between parents and programs. What do parents want when it comes to biting? The Child Care Council has found that parents want two things:

1. They want programs and providers to take biting as seriously as they do.
2. They want the biting to stop.

Parents who call the Child Care Council about biting in their children's programs often say that their concerns are being taken lightly. We have found that parents are upset when programs calmly explain biting in terms of "normal toddler development." To parents, saying that something is normal often comes across as saying something is to be expected and tolerated. This is upsetting for parents because biting is not something *they* expected, and they most certainly do not want to tolerate anything that hurts their children.

The Child Care Council often hears from parents, "My child is being bitten, and the teachers and the director don't even care." Teachers who have cared for toddlers for many years have probably dealt with hundreds of biting incidents. Over the years they have probably developed effective techniques to address biting. They may also have worked very hard to put everything they have learned about biting into explanations and information for parents. Sometimes the very words they have carefully chosen to inform and reassure parents may be interpreted by parents as "not taking the biting seriously." When teachers talk with parents about biting, they must make sure that they express genuine regret about it and that they recognize and acknowledge parents' shock, pain, and (sometimes) their outrage.

Parents also report that when biting becomes an ongoing problem, teachers and directors tell parents, "We're handling it; we're taking care of it," but offer no specific information on how they are taking care of it. When parents don't see any changes in either the program or the amount of biting, they suspect that in reality nothing is being done. Then they feel that the program is either unable or unwilling to address the biting. When parents lose confidence in the program, they may resort to threats of taking their children out of the program or demands that children who bite be kicked out. When parents know that specific steps are being taken to address the biting, they are much more likely to be supportive.

Here is a list of what parents can reasonably expect from their child's program when it comes to biting. Use it as a quick checklist to assess whether you are doing everything you can to support and reassure parents when biting is an issue in your program.

Parents can reasonably expect that a good child care program

- Will put children's safety first and provide appropriate first aid as well as comfort and advice to any child who is bitten.
- Will provide appropriate programming for their toddlers, thus reducing the likelihood of biting.
- Will help children who are biting for any reason learn not to bite.
- Can give parents current information or resources on biting.
- Will take parents' concerns seriously and treat them with understanding and respect.
- Will tell parents what specific steps are being taken to address biting and explain the reasoning behind those steps.
- Will respond to parents' questions, concerns, and suggestions, even when the response to their suggestions is "No."
- Will be willing to schedule conferences about biting with their child's teachers at a time when parents can come.
- Will keep the identities of children who bite confidential to avoid labeling or confrontations that will slow the process of learning not to bite.

On the next page is a version of this list as a letter to parents. We suggest that you use it to let parents know what they can expect from your program. You can also use it as a checklist for parents to evaluate your handling of an actual biting episode. In this case, you would be asking parents to check whether or not you did the things you said you would do. This may help focus parents' attention on program responses that are appropriate rather than on inappropriate responses they may suggest.

Note that in the letter the last item refers to keeping their child's identity confidential if she or he bites. We phrased it this way to help parents identify keeping the child's name confidential as a positive thing. It's easy for parents to feel that the staff is keeping information from them when they keep the child's name confidential. This phrasing may help them identify with the child who is biting, and understand why confidentiality is important in order to stop the biting. You can use either phrasing of this last item in the letter.

Dear Parents,

We are always upset when we experience biting in our toddler rooms. Even though we know that it is not entirely unexpected when toddlers are together in groups, we don't want any of your children to be bitten and we want any child who bites to learn more appropriate behavior. When it comes to biting, here is what you can expect from us:

- We will put children's safety first and provide appropriate first aid as well as comfort and advice to any child who is bitten.
- We will provide appropriate programming for toddlers to help prevent biting.
- We will help the children in our program who are biting learn not to bite.
- We will have current information and resources on biting for you.
- We will have teachers with adequate knowledge and training to deal appropriately and effectively with biting.
- We will take your concerns seriously and treat them with understanding and respect.
- We will tell you what specific steps are being taken to address biting and explain the reasoning behind those steps.
- We will respond to your questions, concerns, and suggestions, even when the response to a suggestion is "No."
- We will work to schedule conferences about biting with your child's teachers at a time when you can come.
- We will keep your child's identity confidential if he or she bites. This helps avoid labeling or confrontations that will slow the process of learning not to bite.

Please don't hesitate to come to any of us with questions or concerns.

Sincerely,

Kirsten Petersen

Johnetta Carmichael

Cindy Chang

Saying "No": When You Can't Give Parents What They Want

Sometimes parents ask for something we cannot or are not willing to give them. Parents often call the Child Care Council to say that all they want is a guarantee that their child will not be bitten, and they truly believe that good programs should be able to give them that. After all, "I pay good money for that child care; they should at least be able to make sure no one bites my child."

While we acknowledge that such a guarantee would be wonderful, we can't give it because we truthfully can't make that promise to parents. The Child Care Council gently tells parents that any program offering such a guarantee is lying to them, fooling itself, or willing to do things to children that they don't even want to imagine.

Parents may also ask programs to

- Keep "the biter" away from their child.
- Give them the name of the child who is biting their son or daughter.
- Kick out the child who is biting.
- Punish the biting child by withholding snacks or activities.
- Let them demand that "the biter" be tested for HIV/AIDS or hepatitis.
- Let them handle the biting situation themselves by punishing the other child's parents.
- Let them discipline the child who bit their son or daughter.
- Suspend the child who bit for a few weeks to "break the biting cycle."

Sometimes these suggestions and demands catch us off guard because, at least to us, they are so obviously the wrong thing to do. But we must take into consideration the emotional nature of parents' responses to biting. In the heat of the moment, parents may want to punish the biting child or the child's parents. Sometimes their demands are an attempt to impress upon us just how serious this biting is. This is especially the case when parents demand that the biting child be tested for HIV/AIDS. Parents may also want to force something upon the biting child or her parents just as the bite was forced on their child.

Parents want decisive action, and they are more than willing to give us suggestions. Teachers need to be responsive and respectful even when they say "No" to inappropriate suggestions. This is not easy, but it is a child care provider's responsibility. Here are some examples of responses that are respectful and recognize the perspective of the parent, but that still do not comply with the parent's suggestion or demand.

> "You would like to have a child who is biting stay home for a few weeks so he can have some 'bite-free' time and maybe break the biting cycle. And the child may indeed not bite during the

weeks he would be out of the program. But when he came back, if nothing had changed here or if he hadn't learned different behavior, he would just start biting again. I want us to spend our energy and time improving our program and helping him learn different behavior."

"Seeing that bite was so frightening. It looks so awful. Now you're worried about AIDS because of the saliva and broken skin. We worried about biting and AIDS, too, so we checked to see whether AIDS is spread by biting. We found out that it isn't. I can give you a copy of that information. This may take care of that worry, but biting is still very upsetting." (Information on HIV/AIDS is included in this book.)

"You're so angry that your child was bitten, and you want me to let you punish the child who bit her. But this is something I am not willing to do. It might make you feel better, but it would not help the child learn different behavior. This is not easy for me to say, because I like to be able to give parents what they want. I would like to tell you what we *have* decided to do about the biting." (This is a good lead-in to sharing the plan you have developed.)

Responding to Well-intentioned Bad Advice

Over the years, members of our task force had gotten a great deal of advice from parents and others on how to handle biting. All of these suggestions are ineffective, some are impossible, and a few are actually cruel. If you care for toddlers, you have probably encountered (or will encounter) these or similar suggestions when there are biting incidents:

- Forcing something into the child's mouth (we have had people suggest vinegar, lemon juice, pepper, soap, and even cigarette butts).
- Punishing the child at home that evening.
- Bribing the child not to bite.
- Biting the child back.
- Having the other child bite back.
- Spanking the child.
- Making the child go to the director's office.
- Popping the child under the chin after biting.
- Keeping the child away from other children, or away from one child in particular.

Occasionally the suggestions are offered out of a desperate desire to do *something.* More often, the advice is well intentioned and people offer it because they think it will work. They may even share an anecdote to prove their point. More than once a parent has said, "Well, my child bit one time. I bit him back, and, let me tell you, he never bit again!" This may be true, but it doesn't necessarily mean that the reason the child stopped biting was because the parent bit him back. It also does not mean that biting children back will stop them from biting in other situations. We have heard from parents who bit their children back and ended up with furious toddlers on a biting rampage.

In order to respond effectively to those who are making the suggestions, you need to know why these are inappropriate responses to biting. Acknowledging the perspective of the person offering the advice is the first step to an effective response. Being able to begin your response in a sincere tone with something such as, "I know it sounds like that might stop the biting..." makes it much more likely that the rest of your response will be taken seriously. Let's take a look at these suggestions one by one to see why they don't work, and why no good program would ever use them.

- **Forcing something into the child's mouth.**
  This may be suggested as an effective punishment. The reasoning behind the technique is that toddlers will stop biting to stop the unpleasant tastes that are being forced into their mouths. Good programs and providers, however, do not guide or correct children's behavior by means that hurt or frighten the child. Toddlers who have things forced into their mouths will most likely be confused, scared, or furious. They will also become distrustful of the adults who did it. This is a prescription to encourage biting, not to stop it.

- **Punishing the child at home.**
  Most parents feel that they should do something to address the biting. They don't want their children to bite, and they feel that they need to make some kind of response. Since they weren't at the scene of the biting when it occurred, they try to punish the child later at home. This may make the parent feel better, but it's ineffective because the child won't connect the punishment to the biting.

- **Bribing the child not to bite.**
  As with punishment, parents usually try bribery because they want to do *something* to stop the biting. And it's important for teachers to understand that parents may really believe it will work. Since adults are able to understand the concept of being rewarded for something they do (or don't do), it is tempting to think that toddlers understand this as well. But toddlers don't make the connection between the action and a promised reward, and they don't make decisions about behavior based on delayed rewards. If a toddler does remember anything about the statement, "If you don't bite, I'll give you a sticker (or some other special treat)," it is likely to be the reward. Toddlers have been known to run to their parents at the end of a day punctuated by bites to excitedly await the promised reward. When parents find out that the child has bitten several times that day, they express surprise that their child still expects the reward.

● Biting the child back.

This seems to be the prevailing advice given by others as a surefire way to get toddlers to stop biting. The reasoning is that if toddlers themselves experience the pain of biting, they'll stop biting others. And, of course, everyone knows someone who claims, "I used to be a biter. Then my mother bit me back and that cured me!" This technique, however, is usually ineffective because what toddlers actually experience is that an adult is biting them for no reason that the toddler can figure out.

Furthermore, biting back is ineffective because children learn behavior that adults model for them. If adults bite, children will learn to bite from them. If adults bite children, they learn that it's okay to bite if you're bigger, stronger, or in the right. This will not stop them from biting.

Finally, the most damaging aspect of biting back is the effect it has on children's trust and sense of security with staff in a child care program. Children need to know that they can trust teachers and that they are safe at child care, which is not true if teachers bite them. Children who don't feel secure are more likely to bite.

● Having the other child bite back.

This is a variation on having the adult bite the child back, and it is ineffective for the same reasons. In this case you are teaching children to bite by allowing (or perhaps even insisting) that a child bite. This suggestion is cruel to both children.

● Spanking the child.

This is yet another technique involving physical punishment to address biting. It is ineffective and damaging for all the same reasons cited above in the section on biting the child back. In addition, most states do not permit corporal punishment in child care centers.

● Making the child go to the director's office.

This technique has actually been written into the plan of more than one child care program, often to show parents that something is being done about the biting. While it does remove the child from the room, it does nothing to address the reason the child is biting or to guide the child in learning other behavior. When the child returns to the room, nothing has changed, including the biting.

● Popping the child under the chin after biting.

Apparently this is sometimes used to train puppies not to bite. It may be suggested on the basis of, "If it works with puppies, it should work with kids." Children, however, need to learn how not to bite, and this technique doesn't help them. In addition, it is likely to frighten, startle, or hurt the child, and damage his sense of trust and security in the child care program. These results are likely to cause more biting. Can anyone imagine toddler caregivers hitting toddlers on the nose with a rolled-up newspaper every time they have an accident while they are learning to use the toilet?

● Keeping the child away from other children, or from one other child in particular.

This is a seemingly commonsense approach to keeping a particular child safe. The problem is that it is almost impossible to limit toddlers to certain areas of the room or make particular children "off limits." In addition, there may be several biting patterns going on, and caregivers could not possibly keep straight who was not supposed to play with whom.

From a philosophical viewpoint, keeping children apart so they can't interact is the complete opposite of what we are trying to facilitate. If we want children to learn to interact without biting, they need the opportunity to play together. When biting is occurring, the task of teaching children how to be with one another becomes more difficult, which highlights the need to do it well. When there seems to be a recurring pattern of one child choosing a particular child to bite, caregivers need to increase their supervision of those particular children, but caregivers can't be expected to keep the children apart.

When responding to inappropriate suggestions, some toddler caregivers like to use a standard phrase such as, "Oh, we're not allowed to do that in our program." This sounds as though they agree that the suggestion is a good one and would try it if it weren't for the "rules" of the program. It's tempting to say something like this because it puts you on the parents' side for the moment. It looks as though you agree, and you are united with parents against "the program." It can defuse parents' anger, or at least keep them from yelling at you about the problem. This approach may seem easier than giving parents the bad news that you don't agree with them, and maybe even getting into an argument.

Unfortunately, siding with parents usually backfires, because it's not really honest. If you helped to make the program's plan to address the biting, and you understand why a parent's suggestion would not work, giving parents the impression that you agree with them is not telling the truth. It gives the parent the idea that even the staff disagree on what to do about the biting. This is confusing for parents, who then don't know whom to believe or what is right for their children. Dishonesty can make parents feel as though staff are not willing to take responsibility for the program's decisions. All of these things can weaken parents' confidence in the program, making it harder for them to trust that the staff are really doing the best they can to stop the biting. In the end, your job becomes harder, because parents who don't feel they can trust the program will give you much less support when you need it.

If you don't feel that you can explain the reasons adequately, or if you are afraid of a confrontation, it's okay to suggest that a parent talk with the director. You can say something such as, "I know it sounds like that would work, but it really doesn't. This is hard for me to explain, but Jennifer can talk about it much more clearly than I can."

Sometimes it's true that caregivers don't agree with the plan that has been made and would like to use one of the methods outlined above to address the biting. If this is the case, it's important to take a look at why you are working in a program that has a philosophy so different from yours. It's still not okay to tell parents that you disagree, because it's not fair to put parents in the middle of a disagreement between you and the rest of the staff. You may need to think about whether it would be better for you to work in a program whose philosophy better matches your own. At the same time, please consider the reasons the techniques listed above are inappropriate. The bottom line is that they don't work in the long run, and they damage children. It is never okay for a child care program to use strategies that damage children to address any problem. Everyone wants the biting to stop, and so it makes sense to use strategies that do work.

Helping the Parents of the Child Who Is Biting

When parents learn that their child has bitten another child, their reaction can range from feelings of shock and guilt to accusations that the program is doing something wrong. It is important to work closely with parents so that all of you can share information that may impact the biting. You also want to let parents know what you are observing in the program and what responses you are trying.

Parents who have experienced both having a child who was bitten and one who did the biting often say that they felt more helpless in the second situation. You may need to offer as much support to these parents as you do to their children. Overall, you want to make sure that you and the parents are working together to end the biting, even though much of the specific work will be done in your toddler room because that is where the biting is occurring. If the biting is also occurring at home, you will want to work with parents to discover a likely cause and then develop a plan to work with the child consistently at the program and at home.

Parents may ask how they can help at home. Here are some suggestions:

- Help their toddler develop language skills.
- Model appropriate ways to express feelings.
- Model caring, empathetic behavior.
- Express disapproval for biting if the child bites at home (this does not mean lecturing, going off on a tirade, or punishing the child).

You may need to explain to the parents just how valuable these actions will be to their toddler, because most likely they will want to suggest punishments. You may need to use the information in this book on responding to well-intentioned bad advice to talk with parents about techniques that just don't work. Parents may also imply that the fault lies with you or the program because their child "doesn't bite at home." Often this is, in fact, the case, because many of the reasons toddlers bite are related to being around more people. Instead of reacting defensively, acknowledge that this may indeed be true, and that the reasons their child is biting may be related to the group setting and the frustration that sometimes comes with it for toddlers.

Helping the Parents of the Child Who Is Being Bitten

Many programs report that this is one of the toughest jobs they have. Most parents react very strongly to biting. You can't assume that because you have always had a good relationship with specific parents they won't be furious with you if their children are bitten. Even the most understanding, reasonable, knowledgeable parents can't help but feel a lump in their throat and a rising level of righteous rage when they see bite wounds on their toddlers. Sometimes it seems toddlers are bitten on the face more than any other part of the body. The bites can appear not only ugly and painful but also disfiguring.

You need to recognize that the first response many parents have to biting is, "Where were you when this happened?" You may feel attacked, but it is not an entirely unexpected response. Parents weren't there to protect their child, and to them it looks as though you weren't either. This is probably not the time to explain how very quickly toddlers can bite. Try responding with genuine regret as you tell them, "I wasn't where I could have stopped the bite. I feel terrible. I don't want any of the children to get bitten."

Here are some keys to an effective conversation with the parents of the child who was bitten:

- Acknowledge and respect the parents' feelings and the depth of those feelings.
- Tell them how you will help keep their child safe (this might include both increasing supervision and helping the child learn to stand up for himself or herself).
- Tell them what you are doing to teach the child who bit not to bite anymore.

At this point parents are likely to give suggestions, make demands, or issue ultimatums that you cannot accept. Unfortunately, you need to realize that your efforts may go unappreciated by parents until the biting stops. You may be trying your very best, but parents are looking for results—often quick results. You can't stop the biting cycle as fast as they would like, which means you need to use all of your skills in working with families. Look to your program administrator for support.

Working with Parents of Other Children in the Program

When you're working with parents during biting episodes, most of your efforts will likely go toward the parents of the children directly involved. Parents of other children in the room, however, are almost certainly aware of what is happening and may need some information and reassurance. There are several ways you can help these parents.

First, make sure they know what you are doing to address the biting in the room and ask them to bring questions they have directly to you. Parents who feel they can get information and answers from you will be less likely to go to other parents to find out what they want to know. If you have developed a plan to deal with ongoing biting, all parents should have a copy of that plan and updates as the plan proceeds.

Second, tell them anything you may be doing to protect children from biting. This is especially important for parents of the youngest children in the group, who may not be able to talk or get around as easily as the older children. Parents may worry that the younger children will be easy targets for others who are biting. Let parents know that you will tell them of any reactions their child may have to the biting in the room. Reassure them that you will comfort their child if he or she is upset by the biting. Ask them to share with you any reactions they notice in their child that they think may be related to the biting.

Finally, give them specific suggestions they can use at home with their own children. Advise them to follow their child's lead. If their child does not talk about the biting, they shouldn't pump the child for information. We don't want to create anxiety where there is none. If their child tells them that a particular toddler is biting in their room, the parent can say, "I don't like biting, and Miss Nancy doesn't like biting. Miss Nancy will tell Adam, 'No biting!'"

If their child expresses concern that someone might bite him or her, parents can tell their child, "I don't want anyone to bite you. You can tell Adam, 'No biting!'" If the child seems quite worried, the parent can add, "We'll tell Miss Nancy that you're worried, and she will help you."

Parents can also help their child learn words that label feelings, and they can model helping, empathetic behaviors for their child to imitate. Toddlers who can express their feelings and have experience with helping and empathy may be less likely to become participants in biting episodes, thus helping reduce ongoing biting.

While these suggestions cannot guarantee that children will never be bitten, they do help parents respond in a way that is appropriate and reassuring to their toddlers.

Other Strategies That May Help Parents

You may want to have caregivers count and record the number of bites they intercept and prevent. This can help parents and staff alike recognize how their efforts are helping reduce the number of bites, and it can be especially useful if you have parents who are keeping a running tally of the number of bites in your program. Keeping track of "saves" is a familiar practice; it is used in both hockey and soccer. Of course, the number of "saves" may not matter as much to parents as the number of bites, and you can't very well say, "Yeah, so there were two bites today. We had five saves, so it's okay." It's much more effective to say, "We did have two bites today and that was upsetting. We're glad, though, that there were five other bites we were able to see coming and stop before they happened." When people are counting, it's good to be able to recognize and acknowledge that "saves" count too. (Use this suggestion cautiously with parents, because saves may not matter much to them and you don't want to antagonize them with more information on saves than on what is being done to stop the biting.)

Sometimes parents are tired of listening to you talk about biting and want another opinion. One program asked two or three selected parents of children in their four-year-old room to talk with parents of children in the toddler room who wanted another parent's perspective on biting. The parents of toddlers felt reassured to hear from other parents who had survived biting in the same toddler program.

When the Outside Community Is Aware of the Biting

Parents are not the only adults who have an interest in biting episodes at your program. You may occasionally find that the entire community seems to know you have "a biting problem." Suddenly people who don't even have children in your program are talking about it at the grocery store, at work, and at community gatherings. It may seem that everyone is an expert on biting, giving opinions or passing judgment on your program and making pronouncements along the lines of, "If *I* were in charge, I wouldn't allow biting in the first place, let me tell you!"

This is most likely to happen as parents talk to their friends and family about the biting and how the center is handling it. And, of course, the people who are the most dissatisfied seem to talk the most. This can certainly hurt the reputation of your program and can also discourage staff. You can hardly issue a general gag order concerning the biting. Telling people that they are forbidden to talk about what is happening will certainly backfire and result in even less confidence in the program. It will also most likely ensure that there will be even more negative comments about the program.

What you *can* do is try to create the message that you *do* want the community to have and then use every opportunity to get that message out to the community. Your message needs to be genuine, positive, and engaging. It must also be true; that is, it must reflect what you really do.

Here is such a message: "Whenever we face challenges at the ABC Early Childhood Program, we work on them in ways that are appropriate for children, families, and staff. And we are willing to take the time to do it well."

This message should be incorporated into the public relations work you do with the community. Do not wait for negative events or publicity and then try to issue defensive statements. Give the community an exciting, positive picture of your program on a regular basis. Write articles for community publications about what the children are doing at your program, and include pictures. Write informative articles for parents about child development. As you are informing the community about your program, work in the message about how you handle problems. You can also include this message in letters and memos to families. Post it on bulletin boards. Put it in the parents' handbook. Use it in newsletters that go home to families. Encourage staff to use the message as a response when people in the community ask questions or make comments about the "terrible biting" in the program.

Staff Members Working Together

During episodes of ongoing biting, parents are not the only adults who are under stress and perhaps feeling frustrated. The caregivers in the room also feel the pressure because they are the ones who are trying to carry out the program, care for the toddlers, work with the parents, and stem the biting. To deal with biting effectively, toddler caregivers need information about biting, support from the administrator and other staff, resources to carry out a plan, and relief when necessary.

This book contains the kind of information toddler caregivers need to understand biting and to choose responses that are likely to work. When biting becomes a repeated problem, they may need help from the administrator and other staff to develop a plan. Other teachers can help by serving as "fresh eyes" to observe the toddler room for program components that may be contributing to the biting. This is an important part of developing a plan to address ongoing biting; caregivers who are in the room every day may not be able to see problems in the program.

Once a plan has been developed, toddler caregivers will certainly need the help and support of the program administrator and other teachers to implement it. The plan may call for a change in the room arrangement or daily schedule, different or less equipment, additional materials, or even additional staff. Caregivers in the toddler room need to know how to request the help (or permission) they need to make these changes. They may need some physical help from other teachers to rearrange the room or remove equipment. If part of the plan involves additional staff, the toddler caregivers need to know that the staff member joining them sees this assignment as a problem-solving opportunity rather than a punishment.

Toddler caregivers need to know that they can count on their coworkers not only for help with tasks, but also for moral support as they take on biting. Without going into great detail, the program administrator should let all staff know what is happening. This can be as simple as a statement such as, "Room Three is working hard to deal with a rash of biting. They have developed a plan that they will be trying over the next two weeks, and they need support from all of us. Please see me if you would like to help."

Other staff can help by asking how the plan is progressing and offering to listen with a sympathetic ear. They can also help by knowing how to respond to parents who complain to them about the biting and how it's being handled. It is quite likely that parents of toddlers in the room with the biting problem also have older children in the program. Some parents may try to draw the teachers of their older children into a discussion of the biting. This is the time for those teachers to support their colleagues in the toddler room by stating their confidence in the toddler teachers and the plan they developed. They should direct the parents to speak directly with the teachers in the room or with the program administrator. If other staff have concerns about how the biting is being handled, they owe it to the program to take those concerns to the administrator directly and privately.

Caregivers who are doing the hard work of addressing biting need to know where they can express their frustration, and how they can get some relief from time to time. This is more difficult than it may seem. Stressed caregivers cannot just leave the room and take a break whenever they feel like it because toddlers must be supervised and ratios must be maintained. Other staff cannot just trot in and out of the room all day to provide breaks because toddlers thrive on consistency and often fall apart when there are too many changes for them.

Programs may have to look for creative solutions to the problem of giving breaks to caregivers stressed by biting. Is there any period during which having other staff in the room might be less disruptive to toddlers? For example, other teachers or a floater might be able to fill in for short periods during naptime. Administrators might use this break time to meet with caregivers and give them an opportunity to talk about how they are feeling, how the plan is working, and what additional help they need. Administrators can also provide some relief by being in the classroom to talk with parents at pickup time, which can be an overwhelming time of day for caregivers.

Finally, if everybody in the whole program is going to know about the biting problems in the toddler room, then everybody ought to be told whenever there is a measure of success. Administrators should publicize the good news, and other staff should offer sincere congratulations.

The Role of the Program Administrator

The program administrator plays a crucial role in addressing biting. He or she develops policies, supports staff, conducts staff development, communicates with parents, and sets the tone for the program. These are all vital when a program is struggling with biting. During a biting episode, the administrator has several responsibilities:

- Make sure program policies related to biting are being followed.
- Support teachers, giving them suggestions and allowing them to vent their frustrations in private.
- Provide appropriate staff development on biting.
- Know where to find additional information, authorities, and technical assistance to deal with difficult biting problems.

- Be available to serve as an observer in a classroom struggling with repeated biting.
- Be available to help develop plans to address ongoing biting.
- Monitor progress on implementing the plan.
- Acknowledge staff efforts to deal effectively with biting and congratulate them when biting subsides.
- Have appropriate information and resources for parents regarding biting.
- Be available to help staff talk with parents who are upset or frustrated.

Because biting is not unexpected, and because it can be very difficult, program administrators need to think ahead of time about how to deal with biting when it occurs. It is much easier to develop policies that make sense for children, families, and the program when you are not in the middle of the stress and frustration of an ongoing episode of biting. The problem is easier to address when policies have already been decided and an action plan is ready for implementation. And when staff have specific training about biting, they will be more effective in preventing and responding to it. Parents who have seen a biting policy in enrollment materials or in a parent handbook are better prepared for biting to occur. All of this means that when you have biting policies in place before an outbreak of biting, the biting episode is likely to be less stressful for everyone involved. It will probably be less severe, end sooner, produce less friction between parents and staff, and thus be much easier on the program and on the children all the way around.

Biting and plans to deal with it are important areas for staff development of toddler caregivers. Topics should include

- How the program's philosophy relates to biting.
- A review of toddler development.
- Understanding the many different reasons toddlers bite.
- Examining how the classroom environment affects biting.
- Appropriate and effective responses to biting.
- Documenting biting incidents.
- Observing toddlers.
- Creating plans to address biting based on observations.
- Talking with parents about biting.

You can use this book to cover these topics. Staff development seminars will give toddler caregivers the opportunity to consider and discuss their feelings about biting. The behaviors we use with children come from our attitudes, beliefs, and perceptions. If we are having trouble implementing (or even imagining) appropriate responses to biting, we may need to start by working on our attitudes, beliefs, and perceptions.

You also need to prepare parents for the possibility of biting. This is a little more difficult than preparing staff, because you can hardly send a letter to parents that tells them to expect that their child will be bitten in your program. What you *can* do is incorporate biting information in a memo or handbook that welcomes parents who are new to the toddler room(s). This memo or handbook could contain information on many aspects of the program, such as activities, schedule, staff, and so on. The information you provide for parents should focus on the specific steps your program will take when biting occurs. Specifics become very important to parents when their child has been bitten. The steps would, of course, reflect the decisions and plans you made as a staff. Developing this biting information for parents is important because it makes you review the steps you take and consider how they will sound to parents. Although we urge you to develop your own information sheet that reflects your decisions and plans concerning biting, here is a sample to help you get started.

Along with all the other information we have given you about our toddler room, we want you to know about our response to biting. Biting is, unfortunately, not unexpected in toddler groups but can be very emotionally charged. There are many reasons toddlers may bite. Sometimes the biting is related to teething. Sometimes toddlers bite to express feelings they can't express with words yet. We have seen children bite when they are frustrated, and we have seen them bite in the excitement of a happy moment. No one can predict which children will bite, but we are ready to help toddlers who do bite learn other behavior. We are also ready to give treatment, sympathy, and advice to children who are bitten. Here are the ways we work to prevent biting and how we respond to it when it does happen.

First, we try to program the day to avoid boredom, frustration, or overstimulation. We provide a calm and cheerful atmosphere with a mix of stimulating and soothing, age-appropriate activities and with multiples of favorite toys. We also work to model acceptable and appropriate behaviors for the children, helping them learn words to express their feelings and giving them tools to resolve conflicts with our help.

Second, if a bite does occur, we help the child who was bitten. We reassure him or her and care for the bite. If the skin is not broken, we use a cold pack. If the skin is broken, we follow medical advice and clean the bite with soap and water. If it is likely that the bite may get dirty, we will also cover it to keep it clean. If your child is bitten, we will call you to let you know about the bite. The teachers fill out an incident report, have it signed by our administrators, keep a copy, and give one to you when you pick up your child. We also respond to the child who did the biting. We show the children strong disapproval of biting. Our specific response varies depending on the circumstances, but our basic message is that biting is the wrong thing to do. We help the child who bit learn different, more appropriate behavior, and we let their parents know that there's a problem so we can work together to solve it.

Third, the teachers and administration try to analyze the cause of ongoing biting. We work to develop a plan to address the causes of the biting, and we put all our energy into keeping children safe and helping children who are stuck in biting patterns. When we need to develop such a plan, we share the details with parents so they know specifically how we are addressing the problem.

Fourth, parents are notified if their child starts to bite. We ask parents to keep us informed if their child is biting at home. Children who bite in our program do not necessarily bite at home. But if your child is biting in both places, it is important for all of us to be consistent in dealing with it. Communication is very important in order to help your child stop biting.

We wish we could guarantee that biting will never happen in our program, but we know there is no such guarantee. You can count on us to deal appropriately with biting so that it will end as quickly as possible. We will support your children whether they bite or are bitten. We want the best for all the children in our program. If you want more information on biting or have any questions or concerns, please let us know.

Developing Policies about Biting

Written policies that are clear and well thought out help to ensure that biting will be dealt with appropriately and consistently by staff. These policies can also serve as a basis for discussing parent concerns and suggestions. If an agency or owner operates several early childhood programs, one policy should be used consistently in all the programs. Include the following in your policies on biting:

- **An introduction stating the program's perspective on biting.**
  The way the program views biting sets the stage for everything else it does related to biting. A program that has taken the time to think carefully about biting is likely to develop, choose, and implement effective strategies to address it.

- **How staff respond to biting.**
  Your policy should state how staff will respond to individual biting incidents as well as episodes of ongoing biting. You may choose to use a general statement, such as, "Our staff express strong disapproval of biting. They work to keep the children safe and help the child who bit learn different, more appropriate behavior. When we have episodes of ongoing biting, we develop a plan of specific strategies, techniques, and timelines to address it. This plan is shared with all parents in the group." This part of the policy may also include specific actions that are prohibited when responding to biting. For example, you may want to add a sentence such as this: "Because we want the biting to stop as quickly as possible, we don't use techniques that alarm, hurt, or frighten children, such as biting back or washing a child's mouth out with soap."

- **How parents are informed about biting.**
  Your policy should detail how parents of both the child who bit and the child who was bitten are informed. It should also include procedures for informing all parents when there is ongoing biting serious enough to warrant an action plan in the program.

● How biting is documented.

Your program should require that all incidents of biting be documented using the program's standard incident report form. Make sure all staff are familiar with a standard procedure for completing these forms, for making them available to parents, and for filing a copy with the program administration. If your program does not have such forms, see the examples on pages 57, 59, and 61.

● The role of confidentiality.

Your policy should include what information concerning biting is kept confidential. Most often, this applies to the name of the child who bit or is biting. The reason for this confidentiality is that we do not want children labeled on the basis of only one of their behaviors. It is, unfortunately, very common to hear a child called a "biter," but we don't hear other children called a "wetter," a "spiller," or a "faller." Being labeled a "biter" defines the child in a negative way, which makes it more difficult to work quickly and positively toward stopping the biting.

In addition, parents may take it upon themselves to chastise the child who bit their child or to try to punish that child's parents. While this may seem very logical, sensible, and justifiable to the parents of the child who was bitten, it does not help stop the biting. Teachers need to be able to spend their time and energy implementing appropriate strategies to address biting rather than monitoring inappropriate actions by parents. Some people point out that parents can often find out the name of the child who bit by asking other staff; sometimes their own child is able to tell them who bit. If they might find out the name of the child who bit anyway, why not just tell them? While parents might learn the name of the child, they are not going to learn it from us. We have chosen to develop a policy of confidentiality based on solid reasons, and we will inform parents of those reasons and request that they honor our policy. Confidentiality is a cornerstone of professionalism in the early childhood field. We cannot practice selective confidentiality and still expect to build trusting relationships with parents.

● What first aid is given for biting.

First aid for biting should be based on medical advice and an understanding of the risk of infection.

Here is a sample policy for you to refer to when developing your own policy. You may decide to use some parts of it and modify other parts.

Biting Policy

Our program recognizes that biting is, unfortunately, not unexpected when toddlers are in group care. We are always upset when children are bitten in our program, and we recognize how upsetting it is for parents. While we feel that biting is never the right thing for toddlers to do, we know that they bite for a variety of reasons. Most of these reasons are not related to behavior problems. Our program, then, does not focus on punishment for biting, but on effective techniques that address the specific reason for the biting. When biting occurs, we have three main responses:

1. Care for and help the child who was bitten.
2. Help the child who bit learn other behavior.
3. Work with the child who bit and examine our program to stop the biting.

Our teachers express strong disapproval of biting. They work to keep children safe and to help the child who bit learn different, more appropriate behavior. When there are episodes of ongoing biting, we develop a plan of specific strategies, techniques, and timelines to address it. We do not and will not use any response that harms a child or is known to be ineffective.

We give immediate attention and, if necessary, first aid to children who are bitten. We offer to put ice on the bite if the child is willing. If the skin is broken, we clean the wound with soap and water. If children are bitten on the top of the hands and the skin is broken, we recommend that they be seen by their health care provider.

When children bite, their parents are informed personally and privately the same day. When children are bitten, their parents are informed personally that day and given a copy of our incident form. When we experience ongoing biting in a toddler room, we develop a written plan with specific strategies, techniques, and timelines to work on the problem. This written plan is shared with all parents in the room.

Biting is always documented on our standard incident report form. It is completed and signed by a teacher and an administrator. It must also be signed by the parent. One copy is given to the parents, and the other copy is kept in the incident report book in the office.

We keep the name of the child who bit confidential. This is to avoid labeling and to give our teachers the opportunity to use their time and energy to work on stopping the biting.

Once a year, toddler caregivers attend a training session on biting. In addition we have current resources on biting available for staff and parents. We encourage parents to bring their concerns and frustrations directly to the teachers.

What about a "Three Bites and You're Out" Policy?

We often find directors, staff, and parents who want to have a policy that kicks children out of the program after a certain number of bites. This seems logical and fair to many adults. The idea is similar to the "three strikes and you're out" laws currently in effect in various parts of our country. This approach has many problems as a policy to address biting.

The philosophy here is that toddlers are solely responsible every time they bite, and that they can make a conscious, informed decision not to bite. We know, however, that many factors can contribute to biting, and not all of them are within the child's control. The environment, for example, is the responsibility of the teachers and caregivers. If the biting were the direct result of an inappropriate environment, would anyone suggest that there be a "three bites and you don't have to pay for a week of child care" policy or a "three bites and the teacher gets fired" policy?

The goal of this kind of exclusion policy is not to help the toddler learn different, more appropriate behavior, but to eliminate children from the program when they don't behave in acceptable ways. The problem is that all toddlers behave in unacceptable ways some of the time—that's part of how they learn how to do what is acceptable. Like all learning, this is a slow, two-steps-forward-and-one-step-back process. Eliminating children who bite from a program stops this process. Teachers and caregivers are no longer charged with helping toddlers, but rather with counting bites. It puts teachers and caregivers in a terrible position, because the policy is "legalistic" in nature, and legalistic approaches create legalistic complications.

For example, what should actually count as a bite? Caregivers may have an eagle eye out for the third bite from a child who is difficult to work with. As soon as teeth are bared, the third bite is recorded and the child has to leave because "that's our policy." For a child who is in better graces, adults may decide not to count a bite that "wasn't really a bite; it was just a little nip." Sometimes biting happens and no one sees it. Must someone be "charged" with the bite? And isn't it likely that a child who has been biting will be the likely suspect?

Caregivers and parents may then also decide that there is such a thing as a "justified bite." If a child bites because another child hit him, should that bite count? What happens when there is a discrepancy in the bite count? A teacher or caregiver may insist that a child has reached the magic number of bites, but the parent is sure the child still has one more to go.

Furthermore, what is the time frame for counting these bites? Three bites in a day? Three bites in a week? Three bites in a month? Is there a "statute of limitations," so that if a child doesn't bite for two months, his previous bite record is erased and he starts over? Does the bite count go with him to the next toddler room?

We know that about half of children bite during the toddler years. A "three bites and you're out" policy might create a contingent of "wandering toddlers," who go from one program where they used up their three bites to another program where the same thing could happen. Instead of having responsive, consistent care, the toddler might have a series of short child care situations. This, of course, would put more stress on the child, increasing the chance that he would bite, while limiting the opportunity for him to learn from stable, loving caregivers how to behave differently.

Toddlers might not be the only victims of this policy. It could also hurt the program it was designed to protect. Enrollment could suffer because parents who must take their toddler out of a program would most likely take older siblings out too. Second, teachers would not be working on developing the skills and creating the environments that effectively address biting. These skills and environments enhance the overall quality of the program and benefit all the children, not just those who are biting.

Biting as a Reason to Exclude Children

Should biting be a reason to exclude a child from your program? This is a touchy subject because it is a frequent request, demand, or even ultimatum of parents. Anyone who has been a director for any length of time has heard something to the effect of, "Either you kick that biter out, or I'm pulling my child out of here." When faced with such an ultimatum, it is certainly tempting to solve the problem by kicking out the child who is biting. This may be especially true when you risk losing several families. It may seem like a simple solution to a complicated problem.

It is not, however, a simple solution. Let's consider the implications first. A program that kicks out a child for biting is indicating that it either doesn't know enough to work on the problem or is unwilling to work on the problem—or both. A program that considers itself lacking the knowledge, skill, and motivation to deal with biting is most likely going to be a program that simply lacks knowledge, skill, and motivation in its work with children. Is this what we are offering parents and children? When we do the hard work of acquiring knowledge, developing skills, and deciding our motivation will be to provide the best for children, our program becomes stronger and more appropriate for children and families. When we excuse ourselves from doing this, our programs become weaker. Programs that have actively, painfully, and successfully addressed biting do not use it as a reason to exclude children. They have lost very few families as a result of their policies.

Let's also consider the child who is biting and his or her family. When a child is biting repeatedly, he needs help to learn other, more appropriate behavior from adults he knows and trusts. This is the most likely way to stop the biting. But it can't happen if he goes from program to program, from adults he knows and trusts to adults who are strangers. Parents may feel that they must either avoid or lie about the reason for leaving the previous program when they try to enroll their child in a new one. Then they can't get the help and support they need either.

Programs often claim to be justified in kicking out a child for biting because they have "tried everything." Very often, "everything" turns out to be a short list of approaches—some appropriate and some not—tried once or twice each. We urge programs to try the approaches in this book, consistently for several weeks. While this will require more effort, that effort will be more likely to pay off.

Sometimes a Child Should Leave the Program

As committed as most caregivers are to the children and families in your program, a few children *will* need a different kind of setting to stop biting. This is determined after trying all other approaches consistently over time. Most likely, biting is not the only problem the child is having in the program. When nothing seems to help, your program should review what it has tried and perhaps ask for outside help in this review. If you conclude that the needs of the child are beyond what even a good program—one with knowledge, skill, and motivation—can provide, you must face that this child might need a different kind of setting or program. Sometimes, for example, a very sensitive child is too overwhelmed by a large infant/toddler program and really needs the smaller group size and multiage character of a good family child care home. This admission comes with regret. When this happens, you need to provide support to the child's parents. Make sure you know how to refer the parent to other resources to find appropriate care for their child. You can start with your local child care resource and referral agency.

Biting and HIV/AIDS

Parents and caregivers may express concern over transmission of HIV/AIDS by biting and may even cite it as a reason to exclude a child who is biting. Our task force contacted AIDS Community Resources, our local source for information on HIV/AIDS. Educators there reported that research, science, and eighteen years of documenting HIV transmission have concluded that HIV/AIDS is not transmitted by biting.

In a 1994 article from *Hospital Infectious Disease News,* a spokesperson for the Centers for Disease Control and Prevention stated, "We have never documented a case of HIV being transmitted through biting. There has to be a certain amount of HIV present in fluid to transmit, and that is not the case in saliva." Most of the research on HIV transmission through saliva is being done in the dental field. Studies by the University of Pennsylvania School of Dental Medicine and the University of Texas Medical Branch in Galveston reinforce findings that HIV in saliva is not concentrated enough to cause transmission.

AIDS Community Resources urges child care programs and providers to get their information on HIV/AIDS from a reliable source, such as the Centers for Disease Control's National AIDS Hotline at 800-342-2437. The CDC also operates a Spanish-language hotline at 800-344-7432.

Documenting Biting

All bites should be documented on the forms your program uses for incidents. Using this form for biting is an indication to parents that your program takes biting seriously and that you are not trying to hide biting incidents. Incident forms also help address the problem that arises when the teacher who is with the child at pickup time is not the teacher who was in the program when the bite occurred. These forms may also be useful when looking at biting patterns, because they contain specific information about the time, place, and circumstances of the biting.

Because biting understandably stirs strong emotions in parents, an incident form left in the child's cubby for parents to discover may be seen as uncaring. You need to tell parents face-to-face about the biting. Your words, tone, and body language should convey genuine regret that their child was bitten. Giving parents this news is not easy, but parents consistently tell us that they want caregivers to be as upset about the bite as they are and to take it as seriously as they do. After parents have had the chance to make sure that their child is all right, you can give them the incident form.

Most programs have their own incident forms already in place. We have included three sample forms if you need one or would like to change your forms. If you have a choice, we suggest using an incident report instead of an accident report. Reporting the bite as an "accident" may be inflammatory to some parents, who may insist, "This was no accident. It was deliberate!"

Incident Report

Child's Name _____ Child's Age _____

Date of Incident _____ Time of Incident _____   AM   PM

How was child injured? What was child doing when hurt?

Were there other children or adults involved? How?

Location and description of the injury

Was any care given on site?   YES   NO   If yes, describe

Was the child's parent/guardian notified? (Circle one)   YES   NO
Was a physician contacted?   YES   NO   By whom?

When? _____ Physician Name _____

Describe any advice given by physician on the back of this report.
Recommendation for future injury prevention:

_____
Signature of Staff Member   Date

_____
Signature of Additional Witness   Date

_____
Signature of Director   Date

Original to Office   Copy to Parent/Guardian   Copy to Child's Folder

Incident Report

Child's Name _____ Age _____

Date of Incident   /   /   Type (accident, illness, etc.) _____

Time of Incident _____   AM   PM

Place (playground, name of classroom, etc.)

Describe Incident

Describe Injuries

First Aid or Other Attention Provided

Parent/Guardian Notified   Parent Signature _____

                               Date _____ Time _____ AM   PM

Signature of Staff Completing Report _____

Signature of Witness _____

Incident Report

Child's Name _____ Date _____ Time _____

Cause and Description of Injury or Accident

Action Taken/First Aid Given

Additional Comments/Follow Up

_____   _____
Staff Signature   Date Report Completed

_____   _____
Parent/Guardian Signature   Date

Other Resources from Redleaf Press

Prime Times: A Handbook for Excellence in Infant and Toddler Programs
by Jim Greenman and Anne Stonehouse
An essential guide to establishing a high-quality program for infants and toddlers.

Beginning with Babies
by Mary Lou Kinney and Patricia Witt Ahrens
An easy-to-use guide containing dozens of activities to help teachers provide developmentally appropriate care for children from birth through fifteen months.

Infant and Toddler Experiences
by Fran Hast and Ann Hollyfield
Filled with experiences—not activities—that promote the healthiest development in infants and toddlers.

More Infant and Toddler Experiences
by Fran Hast and Ann Hollyfield
Filled with over 100 engaging new ways to fill infants' and toddlers' lives with rich experiences that reflect and celebrate each child's development.

Quick Quality Check for Infant and Toddler Programs
by Michelle Knoll and Marion O'Brien
Quick Quality Check for Infant and Toddler Programs is a quick, practical, and easy-to-use method for monitoring and evaluating the quality and consistency of care provided in infant and toddler programs. Designed for center and program directors.

So This Is Normal Too? Teachers and Parents Working Out Developmental Issues in Young Children
by Deborah Hewitt
Makes the challenging behaviors of children a vehicle for cooperation among adults and stepping stones to learning for children.

Practical Solutions to Practically Every Problem: The Early Childhood Teacher's Manual
by Steffen Saifer
Over 300 proven, developmentally appropriate solutions for all kinds of classroom problems.

800-423-8309
www.redleafpress.org